YOUR KNOWLEDGE HAS VALUE

- We will publish your bachelor's and
  master's thesis, essays and papers

- Your own eBook and book -
  sold worldwide in all relevant shops

- Earn money with each sale

Upload your text at www.GRIN.com
and publish for free

Silke Specht

Consultancy Proposal Vodafone Europe

GRIN Verlag

Bibliografische Information der Deutschen Nationalbibliothek:

Die Deutsche Bibliothek verzeichnet diese Publikation in der Deutschen National-
bibliografie; detaillierte bibliografische Daten sind im Internet über http://dnb.d-
nb.de/ abrufbar.

Imprint:

Copyright © 2009 GRIN Verlag GmbH
Druck und Bindung: Books on Demand GmbH, Norderstedt Germany
ISBN: 978-3-656-49140-8

This book at GRIN:

http://www.grin.com/en/e-book/232183/consultancy-proposal-vodafone-europe

Consultancy Proposal

Vodafone Europe

Autumn 2009

Number of words: 2644

Table of content:

1

1. Executive summary

This proposal for Vodafone Europe offers a solution to face the risks for the business caused by the financial crisis as well as by matured markets. To meet the needs of today's customers we provide an experiential marketing campaign.

The core of the campaign is a promotional tour through different countries in Europe. Customers are engaged in the campaign by voting for the locations, at which promotion events can take place, and at the events themselves by getting entertained and educated, by getting an escape from the daily routine and by getting involved in various activities. Beside those "realms-mixture", the concept includes different marketing strategies of sensory marketing. The experiential character that differentiates this promotion event from others is created by keeping the content and the procedure of the event secret from customers until they visit the event.

The finance needed for a successful implementation is enormous, but we also provide possibilities to reduce costs whereever possible. The need for labour is relatively moderate and can mostly be covered by existing Vodafone staff. The time horizon is estimated on a total of five months including a marketing activity before the promotion tour starts. Need for materials is relatively low, as the company already disposes most of it.

The costs resulting from the implementation of the marketing campaign are outweighted by various benefits like an increase in revenues, new contracts and strengthened partnerships.

The team for the implementation consists of three persons: a media designer, an administrative executive and an event manager. All three of them are experienced and have enormous expertise in their field.

We can assure you that this marketing campaign will be a huge success for Vodafone Europe and will help to overcome problems of the financial crisis.

2. Requirements

As you instructed us as a marketing agency to develop a campaign to promote Vodafone in Europe in a new and different way we thought about doing something experiential that relates to you as a company.

Europe must be seen as the main market for Vodafone, where the most networks in various countries are owned by Vodafone or at least in which Vodafone holds a huge share (Licensed Network Operators - Vodafone 2009). In the time of a financial crisis Vodafone has to find ways to fight the cuts in revenue forecasts. As an international operating company customers need to be motivated to do business and to stay with the company (Vodafone Cuts Revenue Forecast - NYTimes.com 2008). New services and special offers may attract some customers to the company, but on the longer run this might not be efficient enough. So the aim of our marketing campaign is to increase Vodafone's international revenues and to attract customers to the company. The target group of the following campaign are private users, as they are easier affected by marketing and still offer a very broad and huge target market.

In the last years customers were overfloated with conventional marketing campaigns from Vodafone. It is normal that they get tired of those stimuli. People react to marketing in which they were personal affected. Consumer-focus and human interaction are some of the main characteristics of experiential marketing. Customers search for personal interactions, relevant messages, authenticity, engagement and innovation and that is what they find in experiential marketing (Lendermann 2006). Therefore we decided to promote Vodafone Europe in a new, experiential and personal way.

To start developing an experiential marketing campaign we thought about what makes Vodafone special for private users? There are many characteristics the company claims to see as their core service, but we decided to focus on internationality, flexibility and simplicity as some more important ones. Those characteristics show that Vodafone is a European actor, that provides services for Vodafone clients in nearly every country of Europe. Flexibility is shown though the various user friendly designs, Vodafone offers to its clients. Complete and compact service packages like flatrates express the simplicity of Vodafone. During the campaign we are going to cover those three characteristics to make people associate them with Vodafone. Internationality will be expressed through the subject of the marketing campaign itself, a promotion tour through different countries in which Vodafone already operates in or wants to operate in the future. People shall get the possibility to vote for the particular location at which the tour will stop. They will get the opportunity to win prizes and experience new and surprising activities like exhibitions, concerts or contests. As this promotion tour will be open to everyone (everyone is able to use Vodafone in one or another way) also simplicity will be expressed.

3. Proposed solution

For our experiential marketing campaign we thought about a combination of sensory marketing (Lindstrom 2008) and the "Experience Realms" approach by Pine and Gilmore (1999). This means we want to attract all five human senses as the experience is much more effective and favourable when sensorial impressions are combined (Lindstrom 2008). In the same moment we will give people something for entertainment, education, escapism and esthetics as the richest customer experiences encompass aspects of all four realms. Of course those experiences need to be in a balance to create an atmosphere in which people are free "to be", "to do" what they want to do, "to learn" what they are interested in, and "to stay" as long as they want to be entertained (Pine & Gilmore 1999).

The core of our campaign would be a promotion tour through different cities in different countries in Europe Vodafone is operating in (e.g. UK, Germany, Italy, Spain, Turkey or Scandinavia).

An acoustic experience may be provided by playing music from various Vodafone stars and concerts (e.g. *Roger Cicero*: Vodafone D2 - Pressearchiv 2007 / Pressearchiv 2009 / Presseservice / Über Vodafone 2007; *Sasha*: Düsseldorfer Jazz Rally 2006: Sasha-Konzert im Vodafone-MobileTV - Aktuelle Meldungen von Vodafone D2 GmbH Düsseldorf Düsseldorf 2006; or *Jan Delay*: Jan Delay « blog.vodafone.de 2009). Further entertainment may be gained through concerts with local stars. The decoration of the event stage should be in the "Vodafone colors" red and white to create some esthetics and a completed picture and to accomplish the memory effect associated with Vodafone. Of course this would be a very welcome opportunity to present new applications and services and to inform people about these as well as let them try those out. An exhibition about the countries Vodafone is operating in could create an educational element. Special foods and fragrances would hereby attract the missing smell and taste sense and thereby complement the whole sensory experience.

Special activities could also include an awarding ceremony for persons that contributed in the online voting for the event destination, the person with the longest travel to the event destination or the person with the most international contacts. Prizes for such awards should of course be Vodafone products or services like flatrates or the like to connect the event to the company even further.

The promotion tour can be combined with further activities of Vodafone, like the launch of a new product or service to reduce costs in the long term. It is also advisable to implement existing staff from Vodafone shops to assist at the events, as they know locals even better and they would also be the contact persons for further business with customers. This is also another possibility to reduce costs, as not as many additional workers need to be engaged.

Before the promotion tour can be realized as described above it is absolutely necessary to have a good marketing campaign with a wide reach. Therefore different media like internet, TV or print media should be combined and used in those countries that might be a destination for the tour. However in this marketing activity customers should not get too many information. They just have to know that something is going to happen and that they can have an influence on where it will happen. The aim is to get people to the events, not to inform them in very detail about what is going to happen at the event. Such a marketing campaign will for sure be very expensive, but as you will see in the next part of this proposal it is worth it.

4. Benefits

The benefits that will be gained from this marketing campaign include increased awareness, new customers and also new contracts. The increased presence of the company in different countries will on the long run also increase revenues. It is also a good and cost efficient way to inform customers about new services and offers. The challenging character of the promotion tour with awards as mentioned before may attract many customers to participate at the event. Also the experiential character of the tour, something that has not happened before, will make people wanting to join the event.

As it may be possible to use existing staff and to stage the event similarly at the different locations cost efficiency is increased.

The event tour will also create positive media coverage and publicity as it is open for a wide public and provides interesting offers, shows and other activities for free.

For the company as such the campaign provides a good possibility to strengthen local partnerships, as local firms will also profit from the campaign, e.g. through guests visiting the location and staying for some days.

Even though it is not one of the explicit aims of this campaign, a promotion tour as is described above might also attract new business customers. Not only do other businesses profit as mentioned above, but also private customers may want to introduce Vodafone into their business as a partner.

For evaluating those benefits against the costs of this marketing campaign also different tools need to be implemented, e.g. for measuring how many new contracts result from the campaign, how was the revenue development in total in the long run, or how awareness developed in countries, in which Vodafone is operating in?

5. Resource Implications

Of course the resources needed to implement this marketing campaign are enormous. To give you an overview about those, we divided the campaign into two main activities: the marketing campaign before the event and the event implementation.

We will start with analysing the resource implications for the marketing campaign that needs to be implemented before the event takes place. To engage an advertising agency might be the easiest solution for this part as they are specialists in their field and their main responsibility would be to get potential customers to look on the homepage that is implemented for the promotion tour and to participate in the voting and/or the event itself.

Also the costs associated with this part of the campaign occur mainly in connection with the agency. We would implement an agreement, so the agency also is responsible for all the materials needed for the marketing and for the homepage and they would get the money for this together with the fee for their service.

The time horizon for the marketing should be three months before the tour takes place, so enough people get aware of the event and can participate in the voting. Additionally, we should calculate one month for the agency to get the media for the marketing in place and prepared. So the work of the advertising agency would start four months before the promotion tour takes place.

The resources needed for implementing the marketing campaign are of course more differentiated and complex. As already mentioned we would use a mixture of existing Vodafone staff from the shops and additional Vodafone staff to ensure a high consulting quality while reducing costs. We would also hire service personal to care for guests, e.g. selling foods and beverages or explaining the procedure of the event. All the technical tasks, like staging the event or securing the music, should be carried out by an agency as they are experienced and can work more efficiently. Also facility responsibles are needed for tasks like cleaning, cooking or ensuring the smooth run of the event. Volunteers could assist with such activities. There is no need to pay volunteers, but at least we should provide food and beverages for them. Finally the whole event cannot be implemented without managers who are involved in the planning, control, implementation and evaluation of the event.

Costs associated with the implementation of the marketing campaign include the salary for the employees mentioned above, material and equipment costs, e.g. for the exhibition, transport costs for personal and material and administration costs.

Not only the materials used for the concerts and exhibitions need be organized, but also food, beverages and merchandising articles that can be sold at the event.

The time frame for the promotion tour should at least cover one month with events taking place each weekend, maybe at two or three destinations at the same time (this would increase costs, as materials are needed in more than one version). During the weeks would be time for the transport of staff and equipment. This solution would also offer the possibility to extend the whole tour when it is successful and you as a company reach your goals.

6. Experience and Expertise in the team

For the execution of this marketing campaign we have a team of three persons.

For the creative planning and implementation of the campaign we have Claudia. She studied Applied Media Sciences and now belongs to the most successful media designer in Germany. Successful marketing campaigns from Calvin Klein, Microsoft and H&M are very good references for her work. In this campaign she should inspire the implementation with her creativity and experience.

Daniel is responsible for the administrative exercises during the planning and implementation of the campaign. He is experienced in working with different Office programmes, worked as accountant for various companies and was involved in the implementation of different campaigns for customers worldwide. For our campaign he is responsible for coordinating ITs, bookeeping and the daily office work.

The team is accompanied by Silke, a studied and experienced event manager. She has got special knowledge in event management, ranging from the planning, above the implementation, to the evaluation phase of events. In different projects she gained experience with international fairs and congresses, staged international events for some of the biggest and most known companies in Europe like Henkel, Unilever and Volvo and also gained experience as a team leader. For our marketing campaign she is responsible for the smooth running of the promotion, so you, as a customer, will get the best service and can be sure that your objectives will be met.

For different phases during the implementation the team will get help from partnering agencies as was mentioned before. We already worked together with those agencies in successfully realising projects for our customers.

7. Bibliography

Düsseldorfer Jazz Rally 2006: Sasha-Konzert im Vodafone-MobileTV - Aktuelle Meldungen von Vodafone D2 GmbH Düsseldorf Düsseldorf (2006); http://www.hotfrog.de/Firmen/Vodafone-D2-GDuesseldorf-Duesseldorf/Duesseldorfer-Jazz-Rally-2006-Sasha-Konzert-im-Vodafone-MobileTV-998; accessed 22/10/09

Jan Delay « blog.vodafone.de (2009); http://blog.vodafone.de/tag/jan-delay/; accessed 22/10/09

Lenderman, Max (2006) Experience the message: How Experiential Marketing is changing the brand world, New York, NY; Carrol & Graf Publishers

Licensed Network Operators - Vodafone (2009) http://www.vodafone.com/start/investor_relations/structure_and_management/subsidiaries.html; accessed 19/10/09

Lindstrøm, Martin (2008) *Buyology: Truth and Lies About Why We Buy*, New York, NY; Doubleday

Pine, B. Joseph & Gilmore, James H. (1999) *The experience economy: work is theatre and every business is a stage*, Boston Mass: HBS Press.

Vodafone Cuts Revenue Forecast - NYTimes.com (2008) http://www.nytimes.com/2008/07/23/business/worldbusiness/23vodaphone.html?_r=1; accessed 19/10/09

Vodafone D2 - Pressearchiv 2007 / Pressearchiv 2009 / Presseservice / Über Vodafone (2007); http://www.vodafone.de/unternehmen/presse/97962_108420.html; accessed 22/10/09